Benedict Arnold

LE GENERAL ARNOLD un des Chefs

Benedict Arnold

BY

MARY DODSON WADE

A FIRST BOOK
FRANKLIN WATTS
NEW YORK / CHICAGO / LONDON / TORONTO / SYDNEY

Eddie's cross still stands on the hill,
And others sleep in Flanders field.
— M.D.W.

Frontis: General Benedict Arnold of the American army as shown in an idealized French painting. The decoration on his hat makes it look British. American officers wore plain tricorner hats.

Cover photo copyright © Northwind Picture Archives, Alfred, Me.
Photographs copyright ©: Ted Spiegel: pp. 2, 6; Connecticut Historical Society, Hartford, Connecticut: pp. 9, 18, 22 top; North Wind Picture Archives, Alfred, Me.: pp. 12, 15, 22 bottom, 27, 31, 36, 38, 41, 45, 49, 51 top, 54, 56; New Haven Colony Historical Society: p. 16; Washington/Custis/Lee Collection, Washington and Lee University, Lexington, Va.: p. 20; Fort Ticonderoga Museum: p. 29; Saratoga National Historical Park: p. 35; Library Company of Philadelphia: p. 40; The Bettmann Archive: p. 47; Collection of the Albany Institute of History and Art, Bequest of Sarah Walsh DeWitt: p. 51 bottom; Collection of the Brandywine River Museum, museum purchase: p. 58.

Library of Congress Cataloging-in-Publication Data

Benedict Arnold / by Mary Dodson Wade
p.   cm.
Includes bibliographical references and index
ISBN 0-531-20156-2
1. Arnold, Benedict, 1741–1801—Juvenile literature. 2. American loyalists—Biography—Juvenile literature. 3. Generals—United States—Biography—Juvenile literature. 4. United States—Continental Army—Biography—Juvenile literature. [1. Arnold, Benedict, 1741–1801. 2. American loyalists. 3. Generals. 4. United States—History —Revolution, 1775–1783 — Biography.] I. Title.
E278.A7W23 1994
973.3'82'092—dc20   94-2574 CIP AC
[B]

CONTENTS

The boot monument at Saratoga, New York, Battlefield celebrates Arnold's efforts in the victory that was a turning point of the American Revolution. He was gravely wounded in the leg, but his name is nowhere on the monument.

INTRODUCTION

*I*n New York State two unusual monuments mark events of the American Revolution.

Visitors to a small chapel on the grounds of the U.S. Military Academy at West Point read the names of generals who led the Continental Army in its fight for independence. But on one of the plaques they see only dates—there is no name.

At the Saratoga battlefield, where Americans won their first decisive battle of the Revolution, a monument in the shape of a boot is dedicated to the general whose bravery turned the tide in their favor. But there is no name.

George Washington called him "the bravest of the brave." His name means something else today.

Benedict Arnold was a traitor.

CHAPTER ONE

Daredevil

"Do it again!" yelled the boys gathered at the mill pond.

Around and around swung the creaking wooden wheel. The short, stocky boy faced his challengers. His light gray eyes flashed against his dark hair and swarthy skin.

The boys gasped as he grabbed one of the blades and it pulled him under. Slowly, the turning wheel brought him up on the other side. Amid cheering, he jumped clear. Nobody called Benedict Arnold a coward.

The Arnold family had once been prominent. The boy's father had been a prosperous merchant sea captain in Norwich, Connecticut. When a son was born on January 14, 1741, Captain Arnold was proud to give his name to the child.

*Birthplace of Benedict Arnold
in Norwich, Connecticut*

At the age of eleven, young Benedict went away to study with Reverend Cogswell. The new student was good in Latin and arithmetic but preferred to play pranks.

Benedict's mother, a religious woman, wrote him long, sermonlike letters. "Keep a steady watch over your thoughts, words and actions . . . . Be dutiful to superiors, obliging to equals, and affable to inferiors," she said. Even when she sent money, she warned him to use it wisely. Captain Arnold didn't preach—he just slipped in extra money.

One day his mother's letter described the terrible yellow fever epidemic in their town. Two of Benedict's sisters died. Only Benedict and his sister Hannah, who was two years younger, were left. Mrs. Arnold ended her letter, "My love to you. Please write. I have sent you a pound of chocolate candy."

The next year, when Benedict was fourteen, things at the family business became so bad that there was no more money for school. Captain Arnold gradually drank himself into a stupor.

Benedict was now 5 feet 7 inches (170 cm) tall, and his athletic ability made him a natural leader. Broad-shouldered and muscular, he was as quick on his feet as a cat. With his powerful legs he could jump over wagons and was a wonderful ice skater. (Later, he became an excellent horseman and an expert shot. The latter skill proved very useful when he got into duels because of his fierce temper. In one duel, however, his opponent chose to fight with swords, thinking that Benedict Arnold would lose. He was wrong.)

Mrs. Arnold tried to keep her son in line, but his wild pranks got worse. Once he led a group that exploded a cannon.

One Thanksgiving the boys rolled barrels of tar to the town green to build a traditional bonfire. When the constable stopped them, a furious Benedict started swinging his fists. The officer marched him home.

Unable to control Benedict, Mrs. Arnold apprenticed him to her cousins, Daniel and Joshua Lathrop, who ran an apothecary shop (a pharmacy). The Lathrops had beautiful houses, servants, fine clothes, and expensive carriages.

The youth learned what money could do. For the rest of his life he worked incredibly hard to get it—sometimes honestly, sometimes not. And he spent it, not only on himself, but on anyone he thought deserved it.

———⟡———

While Benedict Arnold worked for the Lathrops, a man living in Virginia, who was nine years older, served as an officer in the British army. After returning to his farm on the banks of the Potomac, he married a wealthy widow, experimented to improve his crops, and looked after his stepchildren.

George Washington took his role as planter very seriously.
He experimented with new crops at his Mount Vernon
estate, especially after the British began to tax tobacco.

Just nine months before Benedict Arnold finished his apprenticeship, the Virginia planter wrote to London for a long list of things for his wife's children. Eight-year-old John Parke Custis needed clothes, shoes, silver buckles, a leather Bible with his name in gold letters, school books, and writing paper. Six-year-old Patsy Parke Custis got dresses with ruffles, shoes, a doll, and a box of gingerbread treats.

A week later the order was for himself.

Mount Vernon, October 20, 1761

On the other side is an Invoice of cloathes . . . As they are designd for Wearing Apparel for myself . . . I want neither Lace nor Embroidery; plain Cloathes with a gold or Silver Button . . . is all I desire. . . . I enclose a Measure . . . my stature is six feet; otherwise rather slender.

CHAPTER TWO

Merchant Captain

*A*t twenty-one, Benedict completed his apprenticeship and headed for New Haven, Connecticut, to open his own apothecary.

Then, with money the Lathrops had given him, he sailed to London. He bought expensive clothes as well as goods for his store, some of it on credit.

Soon, the citizens of New Haven saw a black sign with gold letters hanging outside a shop on Water Street:

B. ARNOLD
Druggist, Bookseller, &c.
From London
Sibi Totique

A colorized German engraving of a watercolor painting of Benedict Arnold that belonged to the Arnold family.

The last line is Latin and means "For self and for all." For himself, he got a fancy carriage and servants. For his customers, he stocked herbs, dried fruit, balms, fever powders, tea, sugar, and rum, along with watches, buttons, maps, wallpaper, and even the latest novels.

A southeast view of New Haven, Connecticut, in 1786.
This woodcut was used as part of the masthead of the
New Haven Chronicle.

Two years later the store closed because he hadn't paid for things. Arnold plunged into his next career.

For ten years, he was a sea captain, trading horses from Canada for rum and molasses in the West Indies. He was a shrewd trader and soon had the store in New Haven open again.

At twenty-four, Arnold was a respected citizen and became a member of the New Haven Masonic Lodge.

The Freemasons, or Masons, are an organization that emphasizes temperance, prudence, fortitude, and justice.

Fortitude and justice were easy for him. By sheer force of will, he stuck to unpleasant tasks others shunned. And his sense of justice made him one of the first to act against British taxes he considered unfair.

Temperance was a different matter. Because of his father, he never tolerated drunkenness in his presence. But he was never temperate in his actions and made many enemies because of it.

He never gave a thought to being careful. He was absolutely fearless and believed he could do what he set out to do. He almost always did, even against impossible odds.

During these years, he fell in love with Margaret Mansfield, who belonged to a prominent New Haven family. She was twenty-three and he was twenty-six when they married in 1767.

The next year a son named Benedict was born, followed by Richard a year later, and Henry three years after that.

After his second son was born, Benedict Arnold built a magnificent two-story, white clapboard house on Water Street. It had 3 acres (1.2 ha) of fruit and shade trees, a secret staircase, closets, and a special cupboard to hold his many pairs of shoes. The store, with loading wharves, stood nearby.

After he retired as a sea captain, Benedict Arnold built this elegant
home on Water Street in New Haven, Connecticut, in 1773.
It contained a secret staircase and a special cupboard for his many shoes.

Benedict Arnold became rich, but his temper led to duels. One was with a sea captain who said insulting things when Arnold skipped the customary visit among captains in foreign ports. Arnold had no time for such things as he hurried to unload. The first ship at the next port would get better prices.

He loved his family, though, and while he was at sea, complained to his wife about not writing. "You have wrote me only once when there has been so many opportunities . . . you cannot imagine how anxious I am to see you." The homesick sea captain still didn't get a letter.

As Arnold's years at sea came to an end, troubled times lay ahead. England had to pay for a costly colonial war, and the taxes they placed on the colonists outraged Benedict Arnold and many other Americans.

⟶⟶•⟵⟵

In Virginia, the tall plantation owner had much in common with the Connecticut merchant captain. Not only were they both Freemasons, but they also loved horses and nice clothes, and agreed in politics.

George Washington, now a member of the Virginia House of Burgesses, joined an association that refused to pay taxes. He made this clear when he placed another order to England.

George Washington, age 40, in the uniform of a colonel in the Virginia Militia. The picture was painted by famous artist Charles Wilson Peale in 1772.

Mount Vernon, July 25, 1769
But if there are any Articles . . . (Paper only excepted) which are Tax'd by Act of Parliament . . . , it is my express desire and request, that they may not be sent, as I have very heartly enterd into an Association . . . not to Import any Article . . . until the said Act or Acts are repeal'd. I am therefore particular in mentioning this matter as I am fully determined to adhere religiously to it.

CHAPTER THREE

Colonial Patriot

*B*enedict Arnold knew how to avoid paying taxes on goods his ships carried. Like many captains, he considered his actions patriotic. And Arnold was willing to back up his resistance with violence when he felt the situation called for it. For example, he led a mob that tarred and feathered a man who informed on him.

He was in his mid-thirties when sixty-five New Haven "gentlemen of influence and respectability" banded together to form a militia. On March 15, 1775, the Footguards, in scarlet coats with silver buttons, elected Benedict Arnold their captain.

In a matter of weeks the British fired on Americans at Lexington and Concord. Arnold ordered out the

Arnold and his handsomely dressed minutemen arrived too late to take part in the Battle of Lexington that started the American Revolution, but while in Boston he received a commission to capture Fort Ticonderoga in New York State.

Attacking at dawn, Ethan Allen, in his green coat with gold trim, roused the British commander at Fort Ticonderoga out of bed and demanded surrender. Arnold was insulted when the British officer ignored him and offered his sword to Allen.

Footguards. They arrived in Lexington too late to help but made such an impression that they were sent to return the body of a British soldier.

On the way to Boston, Benedict Arnold learned there were cannons at Fort Ticonderoga. He asked the Massachusetts leaders to let him capture the fort on the southern end of Lake Champlain, and they agreed.

When he discovered that Ethan Allen and his Green Mountain Boys were on the same mission, he raced ahead and caught up not far from their target. The short, bristly, proud captain in his scarlet coat stood toe to toe with the tall Vermonter dressed in a green coat with huge gold epaulets.

Allen's rowdy men laughed when Arnold waved his commission, but Ethan Allen couldn't ignore the paper. The two raced side by side into the fort. Benedict Arnold waited stiffly to receive the sword of the surrendering commander. Instead, it was handed to Allen. This snub was the first in a long line of blows to Arnold's pride.

Congress sent a new commander to take his place. Then a committee from Massachusetts came to investigate Arnold's actions. In addition to the controversy about who was commander, they wanted him to account for his expenses, which were ten times the amount they had authorized.

Furious at all the indignities he had suffered, he shut the committee out and wrote a scorching reply. Their charges were, he said, "a very plain intimation that the Congress are dubious of my rectitude or abilities, which is sufficient inducement for me to decline serving them longer."

He resigned his commission and started home. On the way, he received news that his wife had died.

<hr/>

While Benedict Arnold was enduring insults, George Washington was receiving the highest honor of his country. Just one day before Arnold's wife died, George Washington wrote to Martha.

Philadelphia, June 18, 1775

My Dearest: I am now set down to write to you on a subject, which fills me with inexpressible concern . . . when I reflect upon the uneasiness I know it will give you. . . . [T]he whole army raised for the defence of the American cause shall be put under my care. . . . It was utterly out of my power to refuse this appointment, without exposing my character to such censures, as would have reflected dishonor upon myself.

CHAPTER FOUR

Continental Army Officer

*B*enedict Arnold didn't stay in New Haven long. In August 1775 he left his sister Hannah, who never married, in charge of his store and children and went to George Washington with a plan to capture Quebec. According to the map he had, they could march through the Maine wilderness, using rivers most of the way. "We shall be able to perform the march in twenty days," he told Washington.

Arnold's troops left in early September. For forty-five days the soldiers endured incredible hardships. They carried the heavy boats around stretches of choked rivers. The men were mired in swamps and got lost because the map was wrong. They suffered through ice and snow. Food spoiled and finally became so scarce that the men boiled moccasin leather to make broth.

Arnold was everywhere, encouraging his men. Near the end of the march he rushed ahead, purchased food, and sent it back to the straggling soldiers. He paid townspeople to carry those who had fallen in the snow. A ragtag army reached the St. Lawrence River and stood looking across at the immense gray walls of the Quebec citadel.

After a two-month siege, Arnold chose a stormy night to attack. In the fierce fighting, he went down with a shot in the leg. He urged his men on, but the city did not fall.

When British reinforcements came, Arnold retreated to Montreal with his ill-fed, poorly clad soldiers. They had not been paid. Many died of smallpox. Outnumbered, the Americans retreated again.

Arnold hastily arranged supplies for his men, but he left nothing for the British, not even his horse. He stayed until British troops were in sight then stepped into his canoe, keeping his vow to be the last man to leave Canada.

The British tried to follow, but were unable to because they had to take their large ships apart and reassemble them at the north end of Lake Champlain.

During this time, delegates from the thirteen colonies in Philadelphia signed the Declaration of Independence, and Arnold built a navy of his own on the south end of the lake. He hid his tiny fleet behind an island to make a surprise attack from the rear. The British discovered the

After an incredibly difficult march to Quebec, Arnold led his troops in a futile attempt to take the city and was wounded in the leg.

ships and bombarded the trapped Americans all day. Under cover of darkness and fog, however, Arnold slipped his battered ships right past them.

After the British attacked again, Arnold worked feverishly, limping across the deck to fire cannons. Survivors finally abandoned the sinking ships and reached shore in small boats. Arnold kept his men at attention to watch their burning ships sink with their flags flying. Then he marched through the woods to Fort Ticonderoga.

The victory-defeat sent the British back to Canada for the winter. Arnold was a hero. A fellow general marveled, "Few men ever met with so many hair-breadth escapes in so short a space of time."

However, Arnold had made an enemy of John Brown, a veteran of Ticonderoga and the Canadian fight. Brown accused Arnold of plundering supplies for his own use.

Arnold admitted that he took supplies from Montreal merchants for his troops, but he had notified his commander and then ordered strict accounting so that the goods could be paid for later. The man who was in charge of the supplies, however, did not protect them.

Arnold had paid for many things himself, but Congress would not repay him without receipts, which had been lost and captured by the enemy in the chaos. Two centuries later the captured ledgers were found in a library in Quebec.

Fort Ticonderoga, on Lake Champlain, was important to the success of the Americans on the western front. The fort changed hands several times during the Revolutionary War.

Arnold went to Boston to raise troops. While there he fell in love with sixteen-year-old Elizabeth Deblois. He sent her a trunk full of dresses, but she returned them. Miss Deblois had no intention of marrying a thirty-six-year-old man.

But the army's rebuff was worse. Congress promoted five officers to major general. All were younger and below Arnold in rank.

He sent Washington an indignant letter. The snub was Congress's "very civil way of requesting my resignation, as unqualified for the office I hold. . . . When I entered the service of my country my character was unimpeached. I have sacrificed my interest, ease and happiness in her cause."

Washington had not been consulted about the promotions. With soldiers deserting and officers resigning, he needed Arnold. He tried to soothe things. "The promotion which was due to your seniority was not overlooked for want of merit in you," he explained.

Arnold was ready to resign. However, he instead raced to Danbury, Connecticut, to fight off a British attack. On two successive days the horses he rode were killed. His tremendous courage at the head of the troops rallied the Americans.

Arnold was a hero, but on April 12, 1777, John Brown published a handbill with thirteen accusations. Congress, however, dismissed Brown's charges, ordered a

This engraving of Benedict Arnold, based on a drawing by Swiss artist Pierre Du Simitiére, was done in Philadelphia, probably in 1779. Arnold sat for the portrait at about the time he married Peggy Shippen.

new horse for Arnold, and raised his rank to major general. But it didn't restore his seniority.

After two years, his accounts were still not settled. Angered that Congress would question his figures, he resigned. "Honour," he said, "is a sacrifice no man ought to make."

⟢⟶ ❖ ⟵⟣

On the same day Benedict Arnold wrote his resignation, George Washington desperately needed an officer to repel an invasion from Canada. The commander in chief wrote to Congress:

Headquarters, July 11, 1777

If General Arnold . . . can be spared from Philadelphia, I would recommend him for the business. . . . He is active, judicious and brave, and an officer in whom the militia will repose the greatest confidence.

CHAPTER FIVE

The General

*T*he Americans faced two advancing armies—General Burgoyne coming from Canada and another force coming east through the Mohawk Valley. They could cut the American states in two.

Congress ignored Arnold's resignation and instead sent him a copy of Washington's letter. Arnold swung into action.

Although he had fewer forces, he disabled the troops coming through the Mohawk Valley by releasing a Tory captive named Yon-Host Schuyler. Indians who were fighting alongside the British believed this mentally retarded man had special spirits that spoke to him. When Yon-Host ran into their camp and pointed to the leaves on the trees to show the size of Arnold's army, the Indians fled. The rest of the army retreated to Canada.

Arnold believed the best way to stop Burgoyne was to stand and fight. His superior officer, the American commander Gates, kept falling back, however. Gates's plan was to lead the British beyond their supplies. After several violent arguments between the two officers, Gates took away Arnold's troops. When the battle finally came, Arnold had to watch from a distance.

Suddenly Arnold jumped on his horse. Waving his sword, he cried, "Victory or death!" and spurred the animal to a gallop.

He dashed into the thick of the fighting, yelling "Come on, brave boys. Come on!" Arnold led his cheering men up a British embankment and spurred his horse through the opening. In the fierce fighting Arnold's horse went down on top of him and a musket ball shattered his leg that had been wounded at Quebec.

The Americans won. On October 17, 1777, Burgoyne surrendered his troops at Saratoga. The threat from Canada was gone, and Congress at last restored Arnold's seniority.

Benedict Arnold refused to let the doctors amputate his leg. They put him in a wooden box so he couldn't move, and he spent a miserable winter railing against them.

In the spring of 1778, he came home to a hero's welcome in New Haven. Washington sent epaulets and a sword knot.

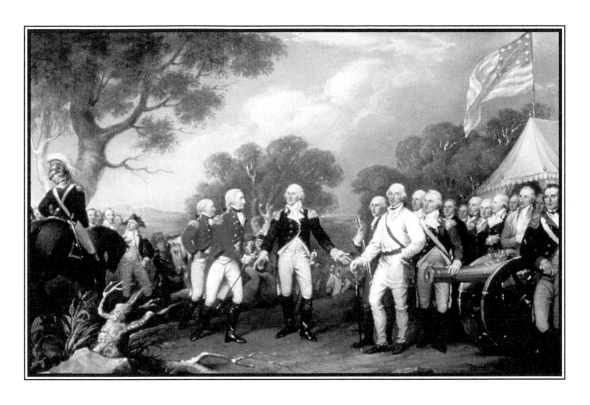

When General John Burgoyne surrendered at Saratoga, due largely to Arnold's heroic action, the British army retreated to Canada. The victory kept the United States from being cut in two.

Arnold also wrote Betsy Deblois again. "Twenty times I have taken my pen to write you. . . . [W]ill you doom a heart so true, so faithful, to languish in despair?" Miss Deblois, however, never married anybody.

Benedict Arnold limped to Valley Forge and signed this oath of allegiance to the United States on May 30, 1778.

Washington requested Arnold to come to Valley Forge when he was able. On May 30, 1778, old comrades watched as the general limped up on his withered leg to sign the oath of an officer in the Continental Army of the United States.

I Benedict Arnold Major General do acknowledge the UNITED STATES of AMERICA to be Free, Independent and Sovereign States. . . . I do Swear that I will, to the utmost of my power, support maintain and defend the said United States, . . . and will serve the said United States in the office of Major General which I now hold, with fidelity, according to the best of my skill and understanding.

CHAPTER SIX

Philadelphia and Disaster

*B*ecause Benedict Arnold's injured leg prevented him from serving on the battlefield, Washington appointed him commander in Philadelphia. The British were pulling back to New York City after months of occupation of Philadelphia.

During the occupation, the British commander lived in an elegant mansion and his officers entertained Loyalist ladies with weekly costume balls, concerts, and comedies.

These affairs were planned by the commander's aide, John André. Twenty-six-year-old André had joined the army to avoid working at his family's accounting firm. He was an artist and poet. He loved music and also wrote and acted in plays. Before leaving for New York with a new commander, André put on a grand party with costumes, games, songs, and contests.

Major John André, the dashing young British officer who knew Peggy Shippen before her marriage to Benedict Arnold, became the contact for the Arnolds to betray the United States.

Arnold arrived in Philadelphia the day after the British left and immediately began making enemies. He moved into the British commander's house. That same week, following Congress's instructions to stop the looting of Loyalists' property, he closed the stores to make an inventory of goods.

People criticized the fact that he had ten servants and that he continued the parties. Arnold icily replied, "I have not learned to make war against women."

At one of the parties Arnold met Margaret Shippen. Peggy was seventeen, the youngest daughter of a Quaker merchant. Beautiful and intelligent, she sometimes threw hysterical fits. Arnold thought she was an angel.

So did the British officers who danced with her and her sisters. "We were all in love with her," said one.

John André had danced with her. He also had engineered a towering hairdo for her and then had drawn a portrait of her in it. However, Peggy never wore the costume he designed for the farewell party. He also designed costumes for her sisters. Mr. Shippen sent his daughters back upstairs when he saw the skimpy outfits.

Later, Peggy's father also objected to a marriage with General Arnold. Arnold wrote in his defense, "My fortune is not large, though sufficient . . . to make us both happy. My public character is well known; my private one is, I hope, irreproachable."

Arnold did have good traits. Just that summer he wrote Hannah to use his money to take care of the destitute children of his friend Dr. Joseph Warren, who had died at the Battle of Bunker Hill.

Arnold's character wasn't exactly irreproachable, however. He made several questionable deals and later had to explain them during a court-martial.

André's sketch of Peggy Shippen in an elegant hair arrangement he planned for her to wear at a party for British officers in 1778, but Mr. Shippen refused to let his daughters attend.

Arnold bought Mount Pleasant as a wedding present for Peggy. In John Adams' words, this estate on the Schuylkill River was "the most elegant seat in Pennsylvania."

To Peggy, though, he wrote words too good to throw away, "Twenty times have I taken up my pen. . . ." Betsy Deblois had spurned them, but Peggy Shippen didn't.

On April 8, 1779, in a quiet evening ceremony in her house, the thirty-nine-year-old general exchanged vows with his beautiful bride. Then he sat with his leg propped on a stool the rest of the evening.

For his wife, Arnold bought "the most elegant house in Pennsylvania." It only added to the stories that he was getting rich illegally.

The Council of Pennsylvania brought eight charges against the general. Congress dismissed the spiteful ones and ordered a court-martial for the others.

Delays in the hearing made Arnold send a wild letter to Washington. On May 6, 1779, he wrote, "If your Excellency thinks me criminal, for heaven's sake let me be immediately tried and, if found guilty, executed. . . . [I have] made every sacrifice of fortune . . . and become a cripple in the service of my country. I have nothing left but the little reputation I have gained in the army. Delay . . . is worse than death."

Washington assured him it would be soon. Arnold responded that he wanted only to rejoin the army "and render my country every service in my power."

———⋙◦⋘———

Even as Benedict Arnold wrote those words, a Philadelphia merchant named Joseph Stansbury was on his way to New York City carrying a very different message from the general to the new British secret service officer, Major John André.

André listened in disbelief as Stansbury explained that a very high-ranking American officer was ready to help the British "either by immediately joining the British army or cooperating on some concealed plan with Sir Henry Clinton."

CHAPTER SEVEN

Road to Treason

*T*ime crawled by. Congress still had not paid Arnold. His business was ruined. His withered leg ached, and he had gout, a painful ailment, in the other one. The only joy in his life was his beautiful Peggy.

The two of them worked out a plan involving a merchant, Joseph Stansbury, who had sold them china. Stansbury was a Loyalist who changed sides as needed.

Stansbury slipped into New York City carrying Arnold's message and returned with the reply—informants were paid according to the value of the prize they delivered. Stansbury also brought back a book to use with a three-number secret code.

The first number stood for the page, the second for the line on that page, and the third for the word on that line. A page marked F meant that fire would make invisible writing show up. A meant acid was needed.

Arnold wrote a coded reply. He insisted on knowing how much he would receive. Then he gave information on troop movements and closed with "Madam A presents her particular compliments."

More months went by. Finally, the messages stopped because there was no agreement on a price.

In December, the long-awaited court-martial began. Benedict Arnold limped into court wearing his buff and blue uniform with epaulets and the sword knot Washington had given him. A 2-inch (5-cm) heel had been added to his boot.

The court was considering only five charges, but Arnold used a mixture of patriotism and sarcasm to present his own defense against all eight.

Three issues were very serious. One charged him with allowing a ship to unload while the stores had been closed. He actually profited from this action but didn't say so. To the charge of selling captured goods, he replied by saying he didn't do it while the shops were closed, but in fact, he had signed a secret agreement to do just that. A third charge, that of using army wagons to move private goods, he answered by saying he intended to pay for them.

After displaying letters of praise from Washington and Congress, he summed up, "I was one of the first that

This pose of Arnold in a uniform with epaulets and sword knot is one of several similar, fanciful portraits.

appeared in the [battle]field, and from that time to the present hour have not abandoned her [the United States'] service." These strong words came from a man who eight months before had approached the enemy about betraying the country.

Confidently, Arnold awaited the verdict. In March 1780 a son, Edward, was born. The commander in chief sent a note, "Mrs. Washington joins me in presenting her wishes for Mrs. Arnold on the occasion."

Three weeks later their friendship would be shattered. The court acquitted Arnold on most of the charges. Congress then instructed Washington to issue a public reprimand of Arnold on two counts.

Washington tried to find a way to save Arnold's pride. On the Orders of the Day, April 6, 1780, he buried the censure among routine information of names of officers on watch and the password. "The Commander in Chief would have been much happier . . . bestowing commendations on an officer who has rendered such distinguished services to his country as Major General Arnold;" but, he added, he found the conduct regarding the ship permit "peculiarly reprehensible," and the affair of the wagon "imprudent and improper."

A week later, the treasury board reported that Arnold's records were hopelessly scrambled. Their best estimate was that he owed the government about $2,000.

With deliberate action, he and Peggy decided to join the British. Arnold explained his reasons in a paper to the

*Peggy Arnold with Edward shortly after they
arrived in England. Only after General Clinton's
papers were examined a hundred and fifty years
later was her part in the treason revealed.*

American people, published after he joined the British army. The general whom Washington trusted set out to betray the country that he had sworn to defend. He hired an agent to sell his things in Connecticut and put the money in a London bank. He went by West Point, a military base that controlled shipping on the Hudson River, to get information about its weak points to send to the British.

Then he limped in to see Washington and asked for appointment as West Point commander, since, he reported to Washington, he "could discharge the duties of a stationary command without much . . . uneasiness to his leg."

Back in Philadelphia, he said good-bye to Peggy and started off, sure that he was getting the command at West Point. He met Washington on July 31 and in stunned silence heard the commander in chief say that he would have command of a troop in the field.

In Philadelphia, Peggy was at a party when a man congratulated her on her husband's promotion. She became hysterical, and everyone assumed she didn't want her husband exposed to danger again.

Meanwhile, Washington puzzled over Arnold's reaction to the honor he had given him. It was totally unlike Benedict Arnold. Two days later, Washington made a new assignment:

Headquarters, Peekskill, August 3, 1780

Major General Arnold will take command of the Garrison at West Point.

West Point, a key military installation on the Hudson River,
was the prize Arnold promised to give the British in return
for money. It is now the United States Military Academy.

CHAPTER EIGHT

Treason at West Point

*A*rnold set up headquarters across the Hudson from West Point in a house confiscated from a Loyalist. He chose Major David Franks and Lieutenant Colonel Richard Varick as aides.

Joshua Hett Smith, a talkative British sympathizer, had a house near King's Ferry, several miles down the river from West Point. Franks and Varick disliked him, but he was perfect to carry Arnold's messages.

Ten days after taking command, Arnold sent Varick to bring Peggy and Edward to him. While waiting for them, he pretended to build West Point defenses but actually weakened them by sending soldiers off to cut firewood.

Joshua Hett Smith's home became known as Treason House after being used for the meeting between Arnold and John André.

Lieutenant Colonel Richard Varick, Arnold's aide, was ignorant of Arnold's plans. He, along with everyone else, was fooled into thinking Peggy was innocent when she began screaming hysterically after her husband left.

Arnold then asked to meet John André in person to make final plans, but their first attempt to meet failed when the British mistakenly fired on Arnold's barge.

The day after his family arrived, Arnold wrote André that he had instructed his officers to conduct a merchant named John Anderson to headquarters. "But if you prefer, I will send a person by boat to meet you on Wednesday, September 20, around midnight."

Immediately afterward, Arnold got word that Washington was coming to King's Ferry Sunday night. His second message that day told the British where they could capture the American leader, but they got the message too late.

In New York City, British general Clinton reluctantly agreed to let André meet Arnold, but he gave specific instructions. André was not to go behind enemy lines. He was not to get out of uniform. And he was not to carry messages. Then, if André were caught, he would be treated as a prisoner, not a spy. Prisoners were exchanged. Spies were hanged.

Arnold went to Smith's house, where Smith was trying to persuade his hired men to row a boat to the British ship *The Vulture*. Slow-talking Samuel Colquhoun objected, "I'm not of a mind to go."

Arnold first tried flattery. When that failed, he threatened to arrest Colquhoun as a traitor.

Reluctantly, Colquhoun and his brother muffled the oars and rowed Smith to *The Vulture*. About 1 A.M. André threw a long blue coat over his scarlet uniform and climbed into the boat with Smith and the Colquhouns.

Arnold waited at the river's edge. In the hours before dawn, the British major and the West Point commander sat in the woods and agreed on final plans for surrender.

As daylight approached, no amounts of threats could make the Colquhouns row André back, so Arnold and André rode to Smith's house. Along the way, they were stopped by a sentry. Arnold gave the password. André was behind American lines.

Sitting in Smith's big stone house, they heard a cannon boom as they ate breakfast. Racing to the window, they saw *The Vulture* pull up anchor and head downstream to get out of range of American guns.

Because getting to *The Vulture* was difficult, Arnold wrote out passes for Smith and "John Anderson" (André) before he returned to West Point. He also handed André detailed information about the fort for General Clinton.

As they left to take a land route back, André disguised himself in Smith's hat and worn-out coat. He kept on his beautiful white-topped leather boots and slipped the plans of West Point's defenses inside his silk stockings. Disobeying this last instruction cost André his life.

Smith went part of the way with André and then left him near British lines. André rode confidently on.

At a bridge just outside Tarrytown, three young men jumped out from the bushes. André first identified himself as British, but when he discovered they were

Arnold's pass for Mr. John Anderson (André) allowed him to pass through American lines on the way to White Plains, stating he was on public business.

Americans, pulled out Arnold's pass. Only one of them could read.

André offered them money and his watch. They searched him and found the strange bulges in his stockings.

The three men took their prisoner and the important-looking papers to an American outpost. When the commander saw the name on André's pass, he started André back to Arnold with an escort.

About then, Washington's intelligence officer arrived and had André overtaken and brought back. The commander wrote Arnold what had happened but sent Washington the papers André was carrying.

André, who did not consider himself a spy, sent a letter to Washington by the same messenger, explaining who he was and that he unintentionally got behind the American lines.

Smith returned to West Point and told Arnold everything was fine.

Early Monday morning, Washington, who had not yet received the documents, sent word that he was coming to Arnold's headquarters for breakfast. He stopped, however, to inspect some fortification.

Arnold was at the breakfast table when the message arrived that "John Anderson" had been captured and the suspicious papers he carried had been sent to Washington.

Arnold bolted from the table. After a hurried goodbye to Peggy upstairs, he threw on his coat and told everyone he was going to West Point. He scrambled on his horse and urged him down the steep embankment to his barge, barking orders to the oarsmen to row downstream to a British ship.

The oarsmen were then ordered aboard *The Vulture* and offered a chance to join the British. "No!" answered one. "One coat is enough for me to wear at a time." Arnold arrested them, but Clinton released them.

Meanwhile, Washington sat in the room reserved for him at West Point. It had been a puzzling morning.

An artist's idea of Arnold telling Peggy that André was captured and he must leave. Peggy soon began to scream that someone was going to kill her baby. Her hysterics gave her husband time to escape.

After breakfast at Robinson House without host or hostess, he had come to West Point. No one there expected him, and no one had seen Arnold. He was appalled at the fort's weak defenses.

Then the daily packet of letters arrived. Washington read the letter from the outpost commander and the one from André. Then he examined the other documents.

Stunned, he looked up at his aide Alexander Hamilton and the French general Lafayette. "Arnold has betrayed us," he said. "Whom can we trust now?"

Benedict Arnold

*B*enedict Arnold wrote to George Washington immediately after reaching *The Vulture*. Claiming he was right, but knowing it was useless to explain, he said, "I have ever acted from a principle of love to my country."

Two weeks later, October 7, 1780, he published an open letter addressed "To the Inhabitants of America." He was, he claimed, trying to stop the war because leaders of the Revolution were "criminally protracting the war from sinister view at the expense of the public interest." The words were an almost exact copy of British propaganda.

Ten days after that, Britain paid him £6,315. Then, for the rest of his life he received a pension of £500 a year. He made more money out of the war than any other American officer.

In addition, Peggy and his sons received annual pensions from the British government. Invested wisely, it would have been enough to live on comfortably, but Benedict Arnold never had enough. He spent lavishly and went into debt.

He stayed in America for fifteen months, fighting bloody battles against his old comrades. Finally, in January 1782, he sailed to England.

This painting, Arnold and His Wife, *by Howard Pyle, an influential illustrator of the late nineteenth century, shows an imagined view of the couple living in exile.*

After briefly enjoying the attentions of the king and queen, the Arnolds were generally ignored or shunned. He bristled at the word traitor and fought a duel with a member of Parliament who referred to him that way.

Still seeking money, he bought a ship and moved to New Brunswick, in Canada, where he had a store. He invested in land and made trading expeditions. After six years of controversy and mistrust, the Arnolds returned to England, leaving Hannah and the older boys with the store.

Arnold continued to sail, and in the West Indies he made one more hair-raising escape, eluding French would-be captors by paddling through shark-infested waters.

Many times he made proposals to lead British armies in combat but was turned down. The most brilliant battlefield general of the Revolutionary War died on June 14, 1801, at the age of sixty.

John André

Major André was hanged as a spy ten days after his capture. During that time he charmed his captors by his conduct and his talent. He faced the gallows with such dignity that spectators wept. A monument marking the place where he died has these words:

He was more unfortunate than criminal,
an accomplished man and a gallant officer.
—George Washington

Forty-one years after his death, his remains were moved to Westminster Abbey in London.

———◆◦◄———

Peggy Arnold

Peggy's hysterics allowed her husband to escape. Everyone who saw her, including George Washington, believed she was innocent. She was allowed to join her husband in New York.

It was not until General Clinton's papers were examined in 1940 that her part in the conspiracy became known. The British gave her a pension of £500 a year for her services.

Peggy's children included four sons and a daughter. All the sons became army officers, and two of them, along with their sister, were noted for their religious devotion and charity.

As long as Benedict Arnold lived, his business ventures kept the family in debt. In the three years after his death, Peggy sold her house and possessions and lived so frugally that she cleared Arnold's debts and provided for her children. She died of cancer at the age of forty-four and was buried next to him in London.

Alderman, Clifford Lindsey. *The Dark Eagle: The Story of Benedict Arnold.* New York: Macmillan, 1976.

DeLeeuw, Cateau. *Benedict Arnold: Hero and Traitor.* New York: Putnam, 1970.

Fritz, Jean. *Traitor: The Case of Benedict Arnold.* New York: G. P. Putnams Sons, 1981.

Lomask, Milton. *Beauty and the Traitor: The Story of Mrs. Benedict Arnold.* Philadelphia: Macrea Smith, 1967.

INDEX

Numbers in *italics* represent illustrations

Allen, Ethan, *22*, 23
American Indians, 33
American Revolution, 19–24
   and treason at West Point, 50–56
"Anderson, John," 52, 53
André, John, 37, 39, 42, 52–55
   hanged, 59–60
Apothecary, 14–16
Arnold, Benedict, 8–13, *15, 31*
   character of, 16–17, 28, 30, 39
   children of, 17, 46
   as colonial patriot, 21–24
   court-martial of, 42–46
   education of, 10
   in exile, 57–59
   homes of, *9,* 14–19, *41*
   as major general, 30, 33–36
   marriages of, 17, 19, 24
   as sea captain, 16–24
   temper of, 17, 19, 23, 46
   treason of, 42–56
Arnold, Hannah (sister), 10, 25, 39
Arnold, Margaret Mansfield (wife), 17, 24
Arnold, Peggy Shippen (wife), 39–41, 43, 46–48, 50, *58, 59,* 60

Battle of Lexington, 21–23
Boot Monument, *6*
Brown, John, 28, 30
Burgoyne, General, 33–35

Clinton, General Henry, 42, 52–53
Code, 43–44
Cogswell, Reverend, 10
Colquhoun, Samuel, 52–53
Council of Pennsylvania, 42
Court-martial, 42, 44–46
Custis, John Parke, 13

Deblois, Betsy, 30, 35, 41

ABOUT THE AUTHOR

"I discovered many years ago that history is not just dates. It is the people who lived the events. That is why I like to write biographies. I meet some very interesting people that way."

For many years Mrs. Wade was a children's librarian, and now she writes for the same age group. She sometimes travels to far-flung places with her daughter, who lives in Boston, Massachusetts, and she enjoys visiting her son in Hawaii. Houston, Texas, is home, but she travels with her husband and gets ideas for writing while doing it.